WE ♥ KAWAII

WELBECK
CHILDREN'S BOOKS

WARNING!

Adult supervision is recommended when glue, paint, scissors or other sharp points are in use.

We recommend adult supervision at all times while making the recipes in this book. Some of the equipment needed to make the recipes in this book can be dangerous if not handled correctly. Please follow the instructions carefully and always ask an adult to help when the instructions tell you to.

Always be aware that ingredients may contain nuts, seeds, eggs, yeast or other allergens, so check the packaging for allergens if there is a risk of an allergic reaction. Anyone with a known allergy must avoid these. Please check any ingredients carefully if you have a known food allergy to avoid an allergic reaction.

Published in the UK in 2024
by Welbeck Children's Books
An imprint of Hachette Children's Group
Part of Hodder & Stoughton Limited
Carmelite House, 50 Victoria Embankment
London EC4Y 0DZ
An Hachette UK Company
www.hachette.co.uk
www.hachettechildrens.co.uk

Text and design copyright ©
2024 Hodder & Stoughton Limited

ISBN: 978 1 80453 675 9

All rights reserved. This book is sold subject to the condition that it may not be reproduced, stored in a retrieval system, or transmitted in any form or by any means, electronic, mechanical, photocopying, recording or otherwise, without the publisher's prior consent.

Printed in China
10 9 8 7 6 5 4 3 2 1

The publishers would like to thank the following sources for their kind permission to reproduce the pictures in this book.

SHUTTERSTOCK
Abracadabra11 16; Alenini 28; Aratehortua 56; ArtVarStudio 31; Shannon Marie Baldwin 60-61, 64; Ballerion 79; Bibadash 27, 59; Anastasia Boiko 57, 58, 71; Caupona 69; Cute little things 35; FrentaN 15, 44-45, 46-47, 65, 70-71, 72-73, 78; Heyneysa 66-67; Jsabirova 69; K. Cozy Bear 48; Olya Koss 49; los_ojos_pardos 40-41, 76-77; ma_nud_sen 3, 4-5, 10-11, 34-35, 46, 60-61; mhatzapa 13, 46-47; Net Vector 7; PhotosKS 50-51; Pigma.S 75; Pogorelova Olga 39; Rebellion Works 44-45; RedKoala 13, 21, 22-23, 47, 71; Elena Sharipova 34; Olena Shevchenko 27; Anastasiia Sorokina 76-77; Spirkaart 52-53; Stock_VectorSale 13, 29, 30; Studio_G 42; Sudowoodo 52-53, 71; Svtdesign 56; Toporovska Nataliia 24-25; Vector Devil 74-75, 78-79; Vividdiy8 2, 65; Wenpei 6-7, 42-43; Yulistrator 25, 27, 39

Every effort has been made to acknowledge correctly and contact the source and/or copyright holder of each picture. Any unintentional errors or omissions will be corrected in future editions of this book.

THIS KAWAII ACTIVITY BOOK BELONGS TO:

....

....

ALL ABOUT ME

This section is all about...you! Choose which super cute animal suits your personality then tick the words that describe you too.

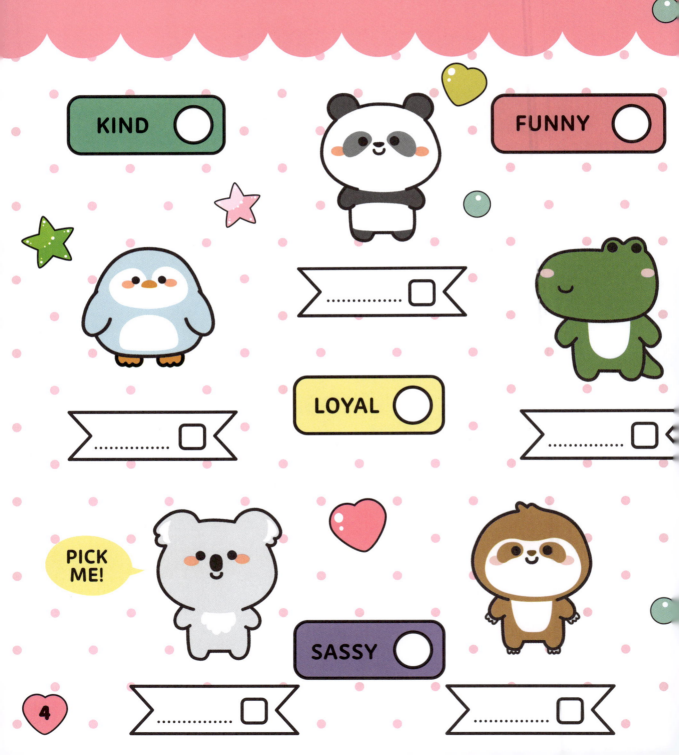

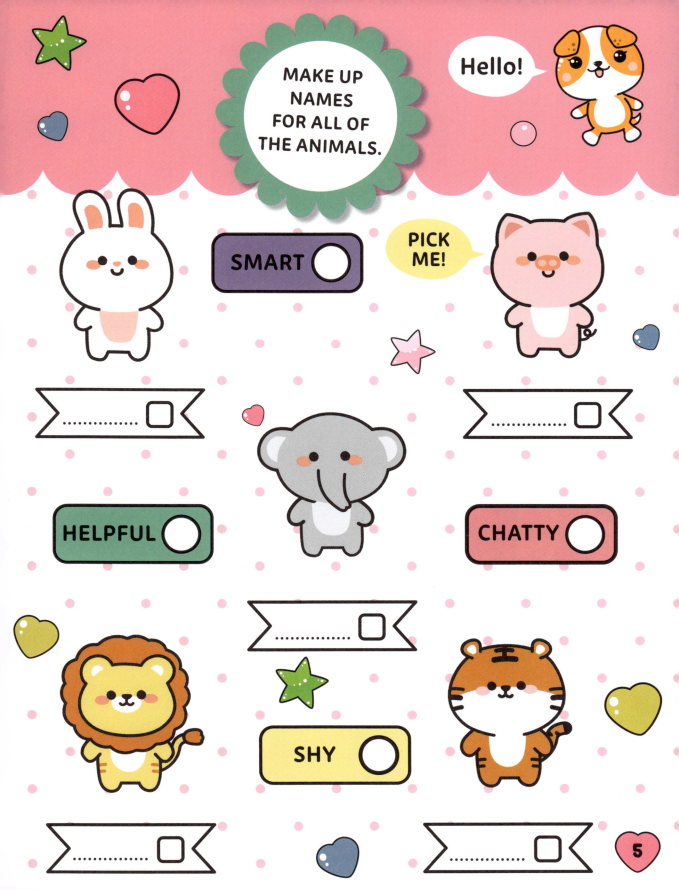

Colouring

HOW TO DRAW A CAT

Follow these simple steps to draw this adorable kitty.
All you need are pencils and paper!

1 Start by drawing an oval shape, like this.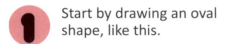

2 Next add two triangle ears and two little feet.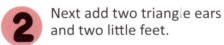

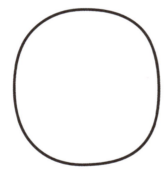

3 It's time to add some personality! Draw its eyes, mouth, and nose.

TRY THIS!

To give your cat a different expression, take a look at the opposite page for ideas.

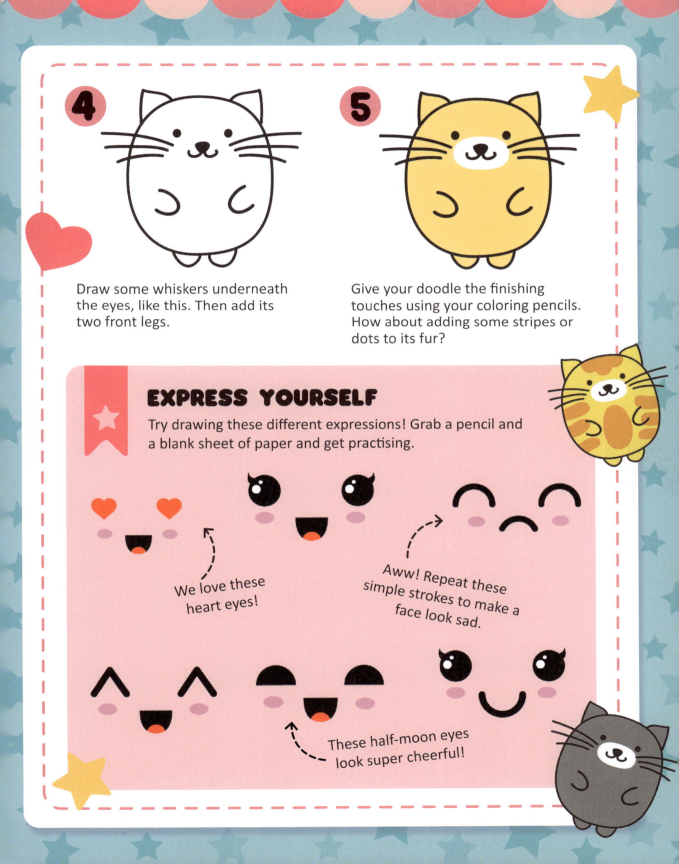

CHATTERBOX CHALLENGE

Who's the lucky one? Fold a cheeky chatterbox and share good news with your besties.

INSTRUCTIONS — You can copy the template on the opposite page or use any large square of paper, then write in your own ideas.

1. Start with a square piece of paper. Fold the top right corner to meet the bottom left corner, making a triangle.

2. Unfold, and then fold the top left corner to meet the bottom right corner. Then unfold again.

3. Fold each of the four corners to meet in the middle, making a smaller square.

4. Turn over. Fold in the corners again to meet in the middle.

5. Next, fold in half to make a rectangle. Unfold, turn your paper 90 degrees and refold into a rectangle.

6. Slide your thumbs and index fingers into the four square flaps and push open.

HOW TO PLAY

Hold the chatterbox closed and ask a friend to choose a number. Open the chatterbox one way then the other this number of times. Then, ask your friend to choose one of the revealed words. Open the flap to discover their special message.

WHAT'S YOUR LUCKY NUMBER?

Move the number your friend chooses.

Move the number of letters in the word they choose.

Your special message.

COPY THIS PATTERN ONTO YOUR OWN PAPER AND CUT OUT.

WHO'S DIFFERENT?

Take a look at the groups of animal pals below. One from each group looks different to the rest. Which is it?

FROG

BEAR

LION

A B C D

GIRAFFE

A B C D

FOX

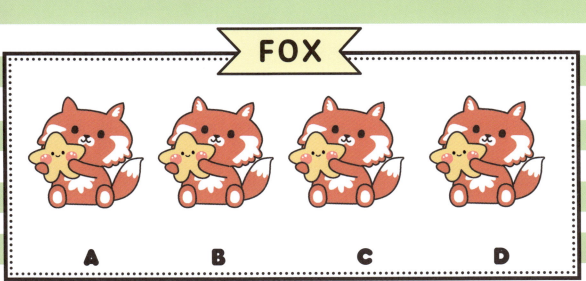

A B C D

BREWING BUBBLES

Design your perfect cup of bubble tea, then color it in!

CHOOSE YOUR CUP
- ☐ **A.** Blue with stars
- ☐ **B.** Rainbow
- ☐ **C.** Pastel stripes
- ☐ **D.** Green polka dots

BASE TEA
- ☐ **A.** Green
- ☐ **B.** Jasmine
- ☐ **C.** Assam
- ☐ **D.** Black

FLAVOR
- ☐ **A.** Vanilla
- ☐ **B.** Passionfruit
- ☐ **C.** Chocolate
- ☐ **D.** Blue raspberry

BUBBLES
- ☐ **A.** Coconut pops
- ☐ **B.** Apple jellies
- ☐ **C.** Strawberry explosions
- ☐ **D.** Rose pearls

STRAW
- ☐ **A.** I bring my own reusable straw
- ☐ **B.** Striped paper
- ☐ **C.** Twisty plastic
- ☐ **D.** Novelty flamingo

HAPPY EVER AFTER

Write a silly short story, using the characters and pictures on this page as inspiration.

One fine day _____ woke up and discovered she'd turned into a _____. She must have eaten a magic_____. The only way to change back was by finding a _____. She packed her bag with _____ and set off to ask the wise _____ for help. On her way she was surprised by a _____ She threw a _____ at it and made her escape. The wise _____ said he would help reverse the spell, but only if she granted him a wish too: to share her delicious _____!

PAWSOME COOKIES

Follow the instructions to make adorable paw print cookies. They're so cute, you won't want to eat them!

INGREDIENTS:

- 8oz self-rising flour
- 4oz softened butter
- 3½oz caster sugar
- 1 egg, beaten
- ½ teaspoon vanilla essence
- Giant chocolate buttons

STEP 1
Ask an adult to pre-heat the oven to 360 F.

STEP 2
In a big bowl, beat together the butter and the sugar.

STEP 3
Sift in the flour and stir in gently. Mix in the egg and the vanilla essence.

STEP 4
Roll the mixture into balls and place on a baking tray lined with non-stick paper. Squash each one down a little bit.

STEP 5
Bake for 8-10 minutes or until light brown in color.

STEP 6
Ask an adult to take them out of the oven and cool for a few minutes.

STEP 7
Stick a chocolate button at the bottom of each cookie.

STEP 8
Break some more buttons in half and push four into the cookie for claws.

TOP TIP!

It's important that the cookies are still soft when you decorate them because it will help the buttons stick. If the cookies are too cool, you could use a blob of chocolate spread or melted chocolate to help the buttons stick!

ALWAYS ASK A GROWN-UP TO HELP WHEN BAKING!

MAGICAL MIX-UP

Copy this mixed-up picture one square at a time in the right order on the opposite page. Then color it in!

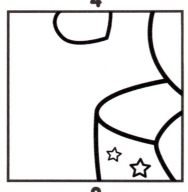

ADORABLE ANIMALS

These cute creatures are the **MOST** adorable. Add some color to the critters below.

HOW TO DRAW...

Follow the steps to draw these little guys. Draw in pencil first so you can rub out any mistakes, then go over in pen when you're happy.

RABBIT

1 First, draw an oval shape with two sausage shapes for ears.

2 Add circles for paws then add eyes, nose and mouth.

NOW IT'S YOUR TURN!

BUDGIE

1 Draw this shape, with a wiggly section in the bottom right.

2 Add a tail, wings, feet, and beak, plus eyes and markings like this.

NOW IT'S YOUR TURN!

KITTEN

1 First, draw a circle for the head and slightly larger circle for the body. Add a tail.

2 Then add triangles for ears, semicircles for paws. Shade in eyes, nose and stripes.

NOW IT'S YOUR TURN!

KOALA

1 Start with a big circle for the head and smaller circle for the body. Add paws.

2 Draw semicircles for ears, and shade in eyes, nose and mouth.

NOW IT'S YOUR TURN!

SWEET SUDUKO

Copy the cute fruit into the empty squares so every row, every column, and every group of six squares feature all six fruits without a repeat.

FUNNY FACES

Who will you be today? Choose an animal or character for a paper-plate mask, then cut out and design your disguise.

Crafts

YOU WILL NEED:

- ★ Paper plate
- ★ Pencil
- ★ Scissors
- ★ Coloring pens or paint
- ★ Glitter pen
- ★ Glue
- ★ Elastic bands
- ★ Hole punch

STEP 1
Pencil the outline of your mask on the plate. Mark where eyeholes need to go and where your nose will peep out.

STEP 2
Ask an adult to carefully cut out the mask shape.

STEP 3
Color and decorate your mask. Add glitter, feathers, whiskers, whatever you like.

STEP 4
Punch a hole on each side, then tie elastic bands in the holes so you can attach it to your ears.

UNDERSEA SPOT

HOW MANY SHELLS CAN YOU SPOT?

Spot 10 differences between these two undersea scenes. When you've found them all, color in both pictures but make the colors different in each picture too!

HOW MANY BUBBLES CAN YOU SPOT?

WHICH CUTE CRITTER ARE YOU?

Take this quiz to find out which kawaii creature you're most like.

WHAT'S YOUR FAVORITE TREAT?
- ☐ **A.** Cookies
- ☐ **B.** Ice cream
- ☐ **C.** Pizza

HOW DO YOU SPEND YOUR FREE TIME?
- ☐ **A.** Playing sports
- ☐ **B.** Drawing
- ☐ **C.** Watching movies

CHOOSE YOUR FAVORITE HAIR ACCESSORY
- ☐ **A.** Shiny clip
- ☐ **B.** Velvet headband
- ☐ **C.** Hair bow

FAVORITE COLOR?
- ☐ **A.** Yellow
- ☐ **B.** Red
- ☐ **C.** Purple

CHOOSE YOUR FAVORITE TIME OF DAY

- ☐ **A.** Morning
- ☐ **B.** Evening
- ☐ **C.** Afternoon

WHAT IS YOUR IDEA OF A PERFECT SCHOOL TRIP?

- ☐ **A.** A visit to the aquarium
- ☐ **B.** Trip to an art gallery
- ☐ **C.** Outdoor adventures

MOSTLY As

You're a . . . dolphin! You're super mischievous, smart, and make the most of every day. Your energy is contagious and you love socialising.

MOSTLY Bs

You're a . . . fox! Sometimes shy but always kind, you love art and are very creative. Happier seeing just close friends, you are loyal and strong.

MOSTLY Cs

You're a . . . panda! Super chilled and calm, you are the steady force your friends often need. You go with the flow and enjoy both playing and relaxing.

SUSHI SOUL MATES

Sushi for two! Draw a line between each matching pair of sushi rolls on the page then tuck in!

CUTE CLOUDS

May we enter? Use the template below to make a cool cloud door hanger, for use whatever the weather.

Use this side if you don't mind people knocking to say hello!

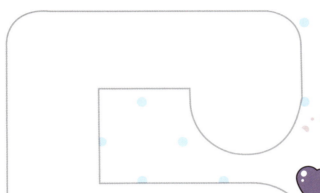

ASK AN ADULT IF YOU NEED HELP USING SCISSORS.

SUNNY SKIES... COME IN

TURN OVER FOR CUTTING GUIDE!

29

KAWAII KOALA

Carefully draw the right side of this cute koala so it matches the left side, then color it in.

KOALAS LOVE CUDDLES!

MEET ME!

Write your name with cute, decorated letters,
then choose the words to best describe yourself.

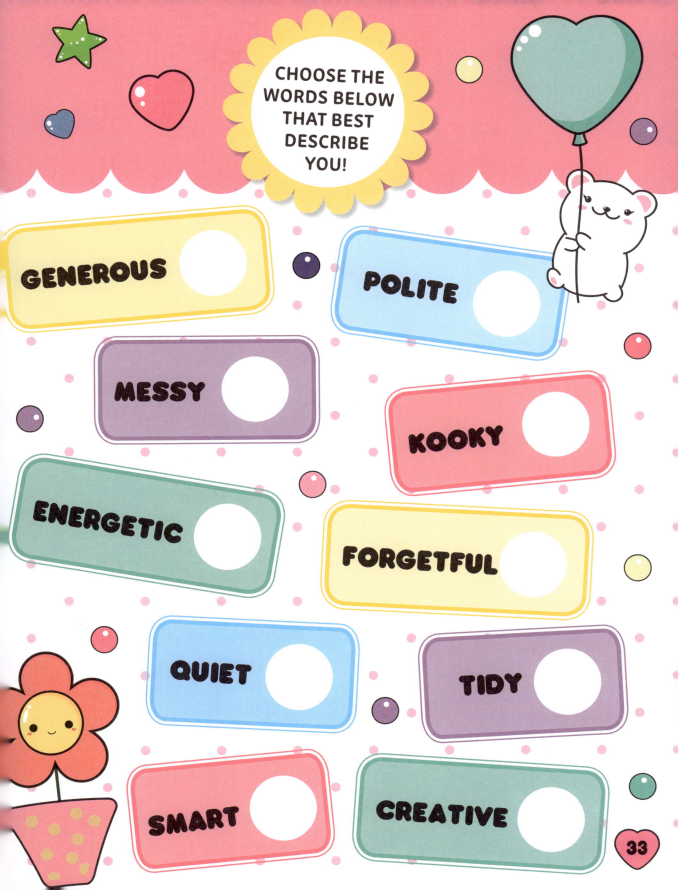